Student Guide to WebCT

INTRODUCTION

Welcome to the Student Guide to WebCT, Version 3. WebCT is a collection of course management tools used to deliver Web-based instruction. Your instructor selected WebCT because of its ease of use and dynamic environment. You do not need any special skills to use this software. If you are new to the Internet, however, you may find that you need to spend some time becoming familiar with your browser.

This guide will direct you through the navigation, features, and functionality of your WebCT course. The guide is divided into the following sections:

- Hardware Requirements and Browser Settings
- The WebCT Environment
- Login and Exiting Procedures
- myWebCT and Course Navigation
- Communication Tools
- Student Tools
- Assessment
- Printing

Each section includes a general description of the features and step-by-step instructions to perform appropriate tasks. While you are enrolled and participating in the WebCT course, you will need access to:

- A computer
- An Internet connection
- A Web browser - Netscape Navigator 4.01 (or higher) or Microsoft Internet Explorer (IE) 4.0 (or higher)

HARDWARE REQUIREMENTS

You can access WebCT using either an IBM/PC compatible or an Apple Macintosh computer. Recommended minimum requirements are:

- **IBM/PC compatible:** Pentium-75 with at least 32 megabytes (MB) of memory; a minimum of 10 MB of free space on the hard drive; a monitor, sound card, and speakers; and a modem for Internet access. Operating system - Windows 95, Windows 98, Windows NT, or Windows 2000.

- **Apple Macintosh:** Power PC (preferably a G3 or an iMac) with at least 32 MB of memory; a minimum of 10 MB of free space on the hard drive; a monitor, sound card, and speakers; and a modem for Internet access. Operating system - System 7.5 or higher.

These are the minimum recommended requirements. With a faster processor and additional memory, you will experience less waiting.

BROWSER SETTINGS

Before you get started with your WebCT course, check your browser to verify that the settings are correct and you have the necessary plug-ins.

Verifying Browser and Plug-in Settings

1. Start your browser.
2. Type `course.com/webct/ckbrowser.htm` in your browser's Address text box.
3. Follow the onscreen instructions to verify your browser settings. Make any necessary changes.
4. Follow the onscreen instructions to verify you have the required plug-ins. If necessary, follow the onscreen instructions to download and install required plug-ins you do not have.

THE WEBCT ENVIRONMENT

WebCT (Web Course Tools) is a Web-based course management and content delivery system. WebCT is user-friendly and requires minimal technical expertise. You have probably experienced many different delivery methodologies in traditional classrooms. The nature of the course and the course content are key factors in how information is delivered. The same is true for courses delivered on the Internet. Your instructor will use a variety of formats to deliver online instruction. As you experience WebCT, you will find a rich set of technology tools to enhance your learning experience.

LOGIN AND EXITING PROCEDURES

WebCT is password-protected. To use this program, you must have a user name (identification) and password. Your first login procedure may be a bit lengthy. Once you complete this process, future logins will be simple and easy.

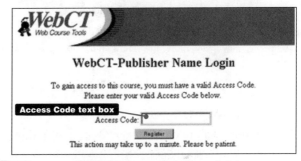

FIGURE 1 Access Code Example 1

Access Codes

Access codes are a string of alphanumeric characters, including dashes, produced by the publisher of the course content. An access code is different from a login user name and password, and is required only the first time you enter a course. The access code is a unique 16-digit number supplied by the publisher, and is located in the envelope on the inside back cover of this guide.

Access codes essentially provide an extra layer of authentication between a user and entry into a course. You will enter your access code at a prompt that looks similar to the ones shown in Figure 1 and Figure 2.

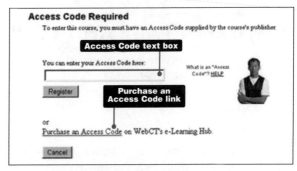

FIGURE 2 Access Code Example 2

First Login

Follow the instructions on the inside back cover of this guide to enroll and enter the course. Use the 16-digit access code that is required to access the course materials located in the envelope below the instructions. For additional information and step-by-step instructions on how to register your access code and log on to your course, start your browser and type course.com/sl/webct in your browser's Address text box.

Subsequent Logins

During your first login, you established your user name and password. Use this user name and password for all future logins.

Logging In

1. Start your browser and access your WebCT course site.

   Your instructor will provide you with the URL.

2. When the Welcome to WebCT window displays (Figure 3), bookmark or add the URL to your Favorites list.

3. Click the Log on to myWebCT link to display the Enter Network Password dialog box.

FIGURE 3 Welcome to WebCT Window

4. Type the User Name and Password you established during the first login session in their respective text boxes. Remember that both the user name and password are case-sensitive.

5. Click the OK button to access the myWebCT page.

Exiting WebCT

WebCT does not have a logoff button. You must close your browser window to exit WebCT. Failure to do so will give others access to your account. Closing the browser is especially important if you are working in a classroom or open lab. To close the browser, click the browser's Close button.

myWEBCT PAGE AND YOUR COURSE

With the login procedure completed, the myWebCT page displays (Figure 4). The **myWebCT** page is a central location where you can view a list of all courses in which you are registered. If you enroll in more than one WebCT course, this process eliminates the need for a separate user name and password.

The page is divided into four sections.

1. The **menu bar** is located directly below the date on the top right and contains links to Change Logon Hint, Change Password, Entry Page, and Help. Click the **Change Logon Hint** link to change your password hint, and click the **Change Password** link to change your password. To return to the Welcome to WebCT window, click the **Entry Page** link. Click the **Help** link for a detailed explanation of all myWebCT options.

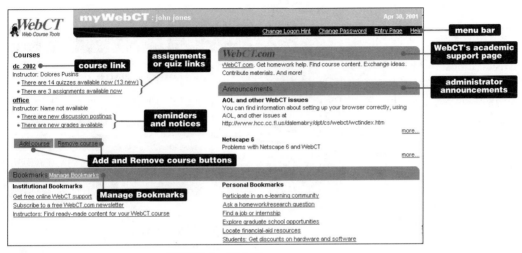

FIGURE 4 myWebCT

2. The top-left section contains a list of all your courses, plus reminders and notices regarding new assignments, quizzes, and other course information. Click the course name to link to the course's Homepage, or click the new mail, new discussions, assignment, grades, or quiz links to go directly to the task. The Add course and Remove course buttons are directly below the list of courses. To add a course, click the **Add course button** and then select the course you want to add. To remove a course, click the **Remove course button** and then select the course you want to remove.

3. The top-right section contains a link to WebCT's academic support page and your school's system administrator announcements.

4. Bookmarks are located in the bottom section. On the left, Institutional Bookmarks contains links to other Web sites created by the system administrator. On the right, Personal Bookmarks includes links to your personal bookmarks. To add, edit, or delete your Personal Bookmarks, click the **Manage Bookmarks** link to display the Bookmarks window. To add a bookmark, click the **add bookmark** link. When the Links window displays, enter a name and the URL for your bookmark. Click Add bookmark and then click Return to myWebCT to return to the myWebCT window. To delete a bookmark, click the check box to the left of the bookmark(s) you wish to delete, and then click the **delete bookmark** link. Click Return to myWebCT to return to the myWebCT window. To edit a bookmark, click the check box to the left of the bookmark, and then click the **edit bookmark** link. When the Links window displays, edit the bookmark. Click Return to myWebCT to return to the myWebCT window.

Homepage

The **Homepage** is your gateway to all WebCT course tools and is the first page you see when beginning a WebCT course (Figure 5 on the next page). The Homepage includes the following features:

- A bar containing links to access MYWEBCT, RESUME COURSE, COURSE MAP, and HELP. Table 1 describes the links on the bar.
- **Breadcrumbs,** or links, that show your location and navigational path within the course.
- A designer-defined **Navigation bar** that you can display or hide.
- An **organizer page** with icons linking to other course navigation components pages and WebCT tools.

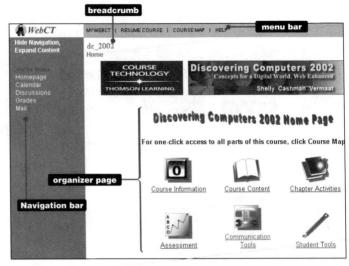

FIGURE 5 Homepage

The Homepage for your particular course may be organized differently with fewer or more icons. Table 2 provides an overview of the standard Homepage icons.

Table 1 Homepage Navigation Bar

LINK	DESCRIPTION
MYWEBCT	Provides a list of courses in which you are registered
RESUME COURSE	Allows you to resume your place in a content module
COURSE MAP	Allows you to view the structure of the entire course on one page; course components are linked, enabling you to go to any place in the course from a single page
HELP	Links to context-sensitive online Help pages

COURSE NAVIGATION

In addition to the Navigation bar, menu bar, and breadcrumbs links, five additional options are available that you can use to navigate through a WebCT course. Clicking an icon on the Homepage links to one of these five WebCT components:

1. WebCT Tools
2. Content Module
3. Single Page
4. URL or Web Site
5. Organizer Page

You navigate in a slightly different way with each of these components. Some may not be available within your particular course.

Table 2 Standard Homepage Icons

ICON	ICON NAME	FUNCTION
	Course Information	Links to general course information such as a syllabus, course requirements, and more
	Course Content	Links to chapter or tutorial content pages
	Assignments and Activities or Chapter Activities	Links to assignments and activities
	Assessment	Links to chapter tests and quizzes
	Communication Tools	Links to Communication Tools, including Discussion, Mail, Chat, and Whiteboard
	Student Tools	Links to Student Tools, including Calendar, Glossary, Drop Box, My Grades, My Progress, Student Home Pages, and Student Presentations

When navigating through the WebCT site using any one of the five components, you should always use WebCT's Home link, or another breadcrumb link to move backwards through the WebCT course. Do not use your browser's Back or Home button.

WebCT Tools

Examples of **WebCT tools** include Discussions, Calendar, Chat, Glossary, Mail, and Search. Detailed instructions on how to use these and other WebCT tools are available in the Communication Tools and Student Tools sections of this guide.

Content Module

A **content module** (Figure 6) includes a number of pages of content such as lecture notes, assignments, quizzes, and multimedia presentations organized into a table of contents. Your instructor generally uses a content module to present sequential content arranged by topics and subtopics. This hierarchical structure also makes it easier for you to find specific course content. You can access the topics or subtopics in any order by clicking a link in the topics list.

The ACTION MENU is located at the top of each page of a content module. Use the buttons on the ACTION MENU to navigate within a content module. Table 3 on the next page lists the ACTION MENU buttons and their functions.

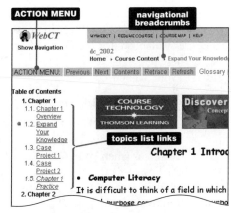

FIGURE 6 Content Module

Table 3 ACTION MENU Buttons

BUTTON	FUNCTION
Previous	Returns to the previous topic in the ordered sequence of topics
Next	Moves forward to the next topic in the ordered sequence of topics
Contents	Returns to the module Table of Contents
Retrace	Takes you back along the path you have navigated through the content module
Refresh	Refreshes or updates the current window

To the right of the ACTION MENU are several additional buttons that link to WebCT tools. The instructor selects which additional tools to add to the ACTION MENU, so the buttons may not be the same for each course. Additional buttons on the ACTION MENU may include Links, Self Test, Quiz, Audio, Video, References, Goals, Glossary, Index, Annotations, Bookmarks, Discussion, Chat, Mail, and Search. These tools might also be located on an organizer page as individual icons. You can find detailed instructions on how to use these tools in the Student Tools and Assessment sections of this guide.

The Content Compiler tool allows you to create a custom collection of course notes from the topics in a content module. After compiling the notes, you can view them on your monitor, print them, or save them to a file on your computer. The Student Tools section provides additional instructions about how to use the Content Compiler.

Single Page

When you link to a **single page** (Figure 7), the page opens in a new browser window. This page has its own set of navigation buttons because it still is within WebCT. Each single page can contain links to other single pages. If additional pages are available, click the Forward or Back button to display these pages. Otherwise, click the Close button to return to your WebCT course.

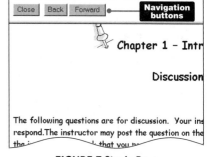

FIGURE 7 Single Page

URL or Web Site Address

Navigating using a **URL**, or **Web site address**, links to another Web site and usually opens a new browser window. Close the browser when you are finished with the page by clicking the browser's Close button. Your WebCT course window will remain open in its own browser window. If the linked Web site opens in the same window, however, use your browser's Back button to return to your WebCT course.

Organizer Page

An **organizer page** is similar in design to the Homepage. The individual icons on the organizer page can link to any of the four components previously described or to another organizer page.

COMMUNICATION TOOLS

Built into WebCT are four **Communication Tools**: Discussions, Mail, Chat, and Whiteboard. Use these tools to communicate with your instructor and classmates. Your instructor can disable any of these tools, so you might find that not all of them are available. As you explore Mail and Discussions, you will find these two tools have several common features.

Mail

Mail is a built-in WebCT communications tool. Within Mail, you can accomplish the following:
- Send and receive messages to and from your instructor and classmates
- Forward messages to others within the course or to external e-mail programs if this feature is enabled
- Search for messages
- Create, delete, or rename folders
- Move messages to different folders
- Compile messages into a single file for downloading

Accessing Mail

1. Click the Communication Tools icon on the Homepage to display the Communication Tools organizer window (Figure 8).

2. Click the Mail icon to display the Mail window (Figure 9).

   The Mail window contains menu buttons and a Mail Folders table. The buttons perform the following actions:

   - *Compose Mail Message: Compose a new message.*
   - *Search: Search for the full name or user name of the message writer, thread subject, unique message number, date the message was sent, or the mail message content.*
   - *Manage Folders: Add, delete, and rename mail folders.*
   - *Manage Messages: Delete or move messages to folders.*

   The Mail Folders table contains four default folders: All, Inbox, Outbox, and Draft. Information about managing folders and managing messages is available on page 13 and page 14, respectively.

Displaying and Reading Mail Messages

1. Click the folder name in the Mail Folders table that contains the mail you want to read. This example uses the Inbox folder.

   The Mail Messages: Inbox window displays (Figure 10 on the next page). Only new, unread messages display by default. Clicking the Show All link allows you to view all messages.

   - *The first line of the message contains the message subject.*

FIGURE 8 Communications Tools Organizer Window

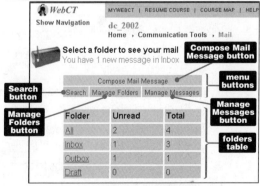

FIGURE 9 Mail Window

- *The second line contains a check box, the name of the sender, the date and time the message was sent, and a NEW icon if you have not read the message. After you view a message, the NEW icon no longer displays.*

- *You can view all of the messages within a particular thread by clicking the linked subject. A thread is series of messages that has been posted as replies in response to another message. Messages are presented by*

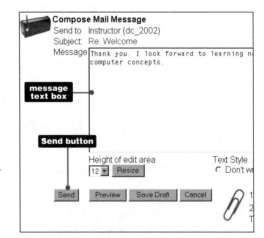

threads. The Unthreaded link allows you to view messages in chronological order.

FIGURE 10 Mail Messages: Inbox Window

- *Clicking the Select Folder box arrow produces a list that lets you switch to another folder.*
- *Clicking the Compile box arrow produces a list that allows you to compile a list of messages, mark messages as read, or mark messages as not read. To use this feature you must first select the message or messages.*
- *The Select all or Select none button selects all messages or deselects selected messages, respectively. Clicking the check box to the left of the sender's name makes it possible to select messages individually.*
- *The Update Listing button displays any mail recently sent.*

2. To read a message, click the linked subject or the sender's name.

   After reading the mail, you can perform these activities: close the message; reply to the message; quote the message in a reply to the sender; forward the message; and download the message.

Replying to a Mail Message

1. Click the folder name in the Mail Folders table that contains the mail message to which you want to reply. This example uses the Inbox folder.

   The Mail Messages: Inbox window displays (Figure 10).

2. Click the linked sender's name of the message to which you want to reply.

3. When the message displays, click the Reply button to display the Compose Mail Message window.

   To include the quoted contents of the message within your reply, click the Quote button instead of the Reply button.

4. Type your message in the Message text box (Figure 11).

5. Click the Send button.

   The mail is sent, and a copy is placed in your Outbox folder.

**FIGURE 11 Compose Mail Message Window —
Replying to a Message**

Downloading a Mail Message

1. Click the folder name in the Mail Folders table that contains the mail you want to download. This example uses the Inbox folder.

   The Mail Messages: Inbox window displays (Figure 10).

2. Click the linked sender's name of the message you want to download.

3. When the message displays, click the Download button to display the File Download dialog box.

4. Click Save this file to disk, and then click the OK button.

5. Select the location on your computer to save the file, and click the Save button.

6. Click the Close button when the download is complete.

Forwarding a Mail Message

1. Click the folder name in the Mail Folders table that contains the mail you want to forward. This example uses the Inbox folder.

   The Mail Messages: Inbox window displays.

2. Click the message you want to forward.

3. When the message displays, click the Forward button to display the Compose Mail Message window.

4. Click in the Send to text box and then type the recipient's mail address. If necessary, click the Browse button to view a list of all members in your class. Click the person's name, and then click the Done button.

   WebCT automatically inserts the recipient's name. To send to multiple recipients, hold down the SHIFT key as you select additional names.

5. Click in the Message text box and type your message to the recipient.

6. Click the Send button.

   The mail is sent, and a copy is placed in your Outbox folder.

   Use the Forward button to forward copies of your WebCT mail to other members of your WebCT class, to your regular e-mail address, or to someone else's e-mail address outside of WebCT. Forwarding e-mail outside of WebCT is available only if your instructor configures your WebCT course accordingly.

Composing and Sending a New Mail Message

1. Click the Compose Mail Message button on the Mail Folders page to display the Compose Mail Message window (Figure 12).

2. Click in the Send to text box and then type the recipient's mail address.

   If necessary, click the Browse button to view a list of all members in your class. Click the person's name, and then click the Done button.

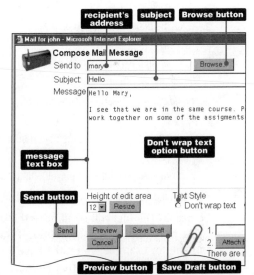

FIGURE 12 Compose Mail Message Window — Composing a New Mail Message

3. Click in the Subject text box, and type the subject of your message.

4. Click in the Message text box, and type your message.

   WebCT automatically wraps the text of messages, meaning that you do not have to press the Enter key at the end of each line. If you have a list of items, however, you may want to disable this feature by clicking the Don't Wrap text button. Clicking the Wrap text button returns to automatic wrapping.

5. Click the Preview button to view the message as it will display when sent.

   Previewing your message is an important step; once you click the Send button, you cannot cancel the command.

6. To make corrections or changes in Preview mode, click the Edit button; otherwise click the Send button to send the message or the Cancel button to cancel the message.

   Both the subject and the body of a message must contain text before Mail will accept a submission. To send the message at another time, click the Save Draft button.

ATTACHMENTS Within Mail, you can send and receive file attachments. If someone sends you a file attachment, you can view the attachment when previewing or reading the mail message or download and save the file on your computer. The **Attach File** button allows you to upload and attach to a mail message any local files stored on your computer. Messages with attachments contain a **attachment icon**. The attachment feature works the same with Mail as it does with Discussions. For instructions about how to use Discussions, refer to page 15.

FIGURE 13 Mail Message Window

Downloading and Viewing Attachments

1. Access Mail, and then click the sender's name of the message you want to read (Figure 13).

2. Click the paper clip icon to display the Attachments window (Figure 14).

3. To view the file in the right pane, click the document name.

   File display is dependent on your browser and software applications on your computer; therefore, some documents may not display.

4. To download the file, click the option button to the left of the file name, and then click the Download button.

5. Follow the instructions for downloading from your browser.

6. When the download is complete, click the Close button.

To display the file, you must have the same or a compatible software program on your computer. If the file is a Microsoft Word document, for example, you must have Microsoft Word or a software program on your computer that will display a Word document.

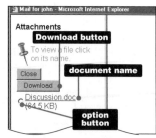

FIGURE 14 Attachments Window

Attaching a File

1. Access Mail and click the Compose Mail Message button to open a Compose Mail Message window.

   Attachment options also are available in the Reply and Forward Message windows.

2. Type the recipient's name, the subject, and your message.

3. Click the Browse button and locate and select the file on your computer.

   There are two Browse buttons in the Compose Mail Message window. To attach a file, use the Browse button at the bottom of the window.

4. Click the Open button to display the file name in the Browse text box.

5. Click the Attach File button to display the Attach Files window.

   The file name and file size display below the Attach file button (Figure 15).

6. Click the Send button to send the message and the file attachment to the mail recipient.

   The mail is sent and a copy is placed in the Outbox folder. You can attach multiple documents to a single message by repeating steps 3 through 5.

MANAGING FOLDERS Use folders to sort, store, and organize your mail messages. Each user has four default folders as shown in the Mail window in Figure 9 on page 9.

- All: The All folder contains all folder messages.
- Draft: The Draft folder contains unsent messages.
- Inbox: The Inbox folder contains messages received from other users.
- Outbox: The Outbox contains messages sent to other users.

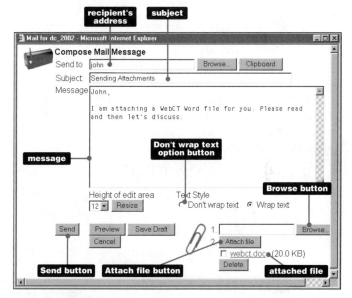

FIGURE 15 Compose Mail Message with Attachment

Adding a Folder

1. Click the Manage Folders button in the Mail window to display the Manage Folders window (Figure 16).

2. Click the Add folder option button, and type the folder name in the text box.

3. Click the Go button to create your new folder.

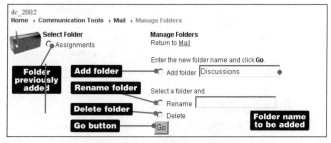

FIGURE 16 Manage Folders

Renaming a Folder

1. Click the Manage Folders button in the Mail window to display the Manage Folders window.
2. Click the option button to the left of the folder you want to rename (Figure 16 on the previous page).

   Only folder names you have added display. You cannot rename the four default folders.

3. Click the Rename option button, and type the new name for the folder in the text box.
4. Click the Go button to rename your folder.

Deleting a Folder

1. Click the Manage Folders button in the Mail window to display the Manage Folders window.
2. Click the option button to the left of the folder you want to delete (Figure 16).

   Only folder names you have added display. You cannot delete the four default folders.

3. Click the Delete option button.
4. Click the Go button to delete the folder.

MANAGING MESSAGES WebCT provides several options to assist with organizing and managing your mail messages. These options include moving a message, deleting a single message, or deleting all messages. The compiling and downloading feature allows you to select mail messages, compile them into one file, and download the file.

Moving a Message to a Different Folder

1. Click the folder name in the Mail Folders table that contains the mail you want to move. This example uses the Inbox folder.

   The Mail Messages: Inbox window displays.

2. Click the Manage Messages button.

   The Manage Messages: Inbox window displays (Figure 17).

3. Select the message(s) you want to move.

   You can select all of the messages or select specific messages by clicking the check box to the left of the sender's name.

4. Click Move to the following folder option button, click the box arrow, and then click the folder name in the list.

5. Click the Go button to move the message(s).

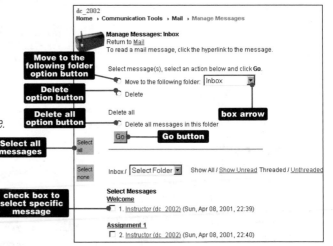

FIGURE 17 Manage Messages: Inbox Window

Deleting Messages

1. Click the folder name in the Mail Folders table that contains the mail message you want to delete. This example uses the Inbox folder.

   The Mail Messages: Inbox window displays.

2. Click the Manage Messages button.

The Manage Messages: Inbox window displays (Figure 17).

3. Click the Delete option button and then select the message(s) to delete.

You can select all of the messages by clicking Select all or select specific messages by clicking the checkbox to the left of the sender's name. You can delete all messages in the folder by selecting the Delete all option button.

4. Click the Go button to delete the message(s).

Compiling and Downloading Mail

1. Click the folder name in the Mail Folders table that contains the mail you want to compile and download. This example uses the Inbox folder.

The Manage Messages: Inbox window displays (Figure 17).

2. Select the order in which the messages will be presented. Click Unthreaded for chronological order; click Threaded for threaded order.

3. If necessary, click the Apply to selected message(s) below box arrow and click Compile in the list. The other two selections in the list are Mark Read and Mark Unread.

4. Select the messages to be compiled in the list of messages. Click the Select all button to select all messages; click the check box to the left of the sender's name to select individual messages.

5. Click the Go button to display the compiled messages.

6. Click the Download button to display the File Download dialog box.

7. Click Save this file to disk, and then click the OK button.

8. Select the location on your computer to save the file, and click the Save button.

9. If necessary, click the Close button when the download is complete.

Discussions

Discussions provide the main structure for group communication, making it one of the more important tools within WebCT. Your instructor may choose to use Discussions in several ways: to ask questions and to facilitate discussions, to post general notices, and to construct public or private topics.

Discussions and Mail have many common features. Within Discussions, students, instructors, and teaching assistants can send, read, and search for messages, and compile messages into a single file for downloading. The main difference between Discussions and Mail is that most discussions are public and can be read by anyone in the class, whereas Mail is private between you and the person(s) to whom you send the message.

Accessing Discussions

1. Click the Communication Tools icon on the Homepage (Figure 5 on page 6) to display the Communication Tools organizer page.

2. Click the Discussions icon to display the Discussions window (Figure 18).

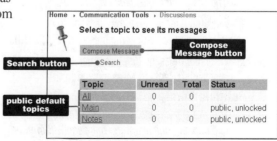

FIGURE 18 Discussions Window

Discussions are divided into different topics that allow your instructor to create discussion groups around particular subjects. Topics can be public or private. Everyone in your course can access public topics, while private topics are available only to the set of students and teaching assistants that the instructor selects. The Discussions page contains buttons and a Discussions Topics table. Use the buttons to perform the following actions:

- Compose Message: Compose a new message.
- Search: Search for a full name or user name of the message writer, a thread subject, a unique message number, the date a message was sent, or the mail message content.

By default, Discussions contain three public topics:

- All: The All topic contains all messages from all public topics.
- Main: The Main topic includes the main discussion area.
- Notes: The Notes topic consists of messages related to a page of content in a content module.

Displaying and Reading Discussion Messages

1. Click the topic in the Discussions Topics table that contains the discussions you want to read. This example uses the Main topic.

   The Discussion Messages: Main window displays (Figure 19).

2. Click the linked user name of the message to read the individual user comment, or click the subject link to read the entire thread.

   Only unread messages are listed; click the All Messages link to view all messages; click the Unthreaded link to view messages in chronological order.

   Messages are presented by threads.

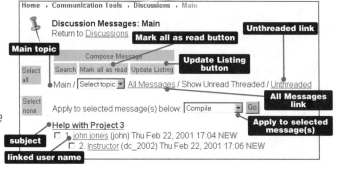

FIGURE 19 Discussion Messages: Main Window

3. Read the message and then perform any of the following activities: Close the message, reply to the message, reply privately to the message, quote the message in a reply to the sender, or download the message.

Replying to a Message

1. Click the topic in the Discussions Topics table that contains the message to which you want to reply.

   The Discussion Messages window displays.

2. Click the user name of the message to which you want to reply and to display the message (Figure 20).

3. When the message displays, click the Reply button to display the Reply to Message window.

   Clicking the Reply Privately button replies privately to an individual message; clicking the Quote button includes the quoted contents of the message within your reply. The Reply Privately button may not be available in some earlier versions of WebCT.

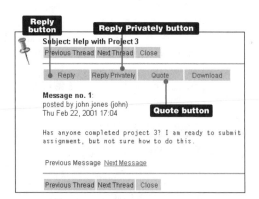

FIGURE 20 Discussion Message Displayed

4. Type your message in the Message text box. (Figure 21).

5. Click the Post button to post the message.

Downloading Messages

1. Click the topic in the Discussions Topics table that contains the message you want to download. This example uses the Main topic.

   The Discussion Messages: Main window displays (Figure 19).

2. Click the message you want to download.

3. When the message displays, click Download to display the File Download dialog box.

4. Click Save this file to disk, and then click the OK button.

5. Select the location on your computer to save the file, and click the Save button.

6. Click the Close button when the download is complete.

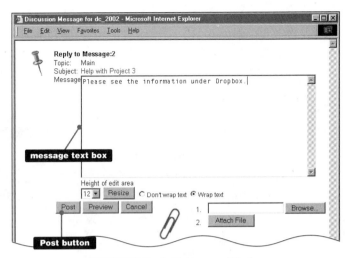

FIGURE 21 Reply To Message Window

Composing and Posting a New Message

1. Click a topic in the Discussions Topics table.

   The Discussion Messages: Main window displays.

2. Click the Compose Message button to display the Compose Discussion Message window.

   The Compose Discussion Message window displays (Figure 22).

3. Click the Topic box arrow and then click the topic to which you want to post your message.

4. Type the subject in the Subject text box and your message in the Message text box. The Main topic is used in this example.

   Blank subjects or messages are not allowed.

5. Click the Preview button to view the message as it will display when posted.

   Previewing your message is an important step; once you click the Post button, you cannot cancel the command.

6. To make corrections or changes in Preview mode, click the Edit button; otherwise click the Post button to post the message or the Cancel button to cancel the message.

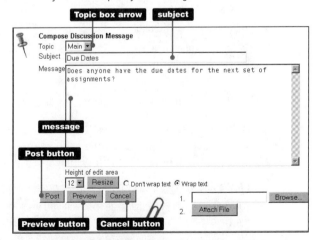

FIGURE 22 Compose Discussion Message Window

ATTACHMENTS Within Discussions, you can send and receive file attachments. If someone sends you a file attachment, you can view the attachment when previewing or reading the Discussions message or download and save the file on your computer. The Attach File button allows you to upload and attach to a Discussions message any local files stored on your computer. Messages with attachments contain a paper clip icon. The attachment option works the same with Discussions as it does with Mail.

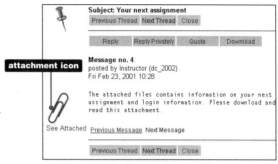

Downloading and Viewing Attachments

1. In Discussions, click the message you want to read. (Figure 23).

2. Click the attachment icon.

   The Attachments window displays (Figure 24). Attachment file names display in the left pane of the Attachments window.

FIGURE 23 Discussion Message with Attachment

3. To view the file in the right pane, click the document name.

   File display is dependent on your browser and software applications on your computer; therefore, some files may not display.

4. To download a file, click the option button of the file you want to download.

5. Click the Download button to display the File Download dialog box.

6. Click Save this file to disk and then click the OK button.

7. Select the location on your computer to save the file, and click the Save button.

8. Click the Close button when the download is complete.

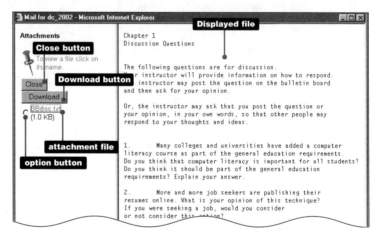

FIGURE 24 Attachments Window

To display the file, you must have the same or a compatible software program on your computer. If the file is a Microsoft Word document, for example, you must have Microsoft Word or a software program on your computer that will display a Word document.

Attaching a File

1. In Discussions, click the message to which you want to respond or click Compose Message (Figure 19 on page 16).

2. When the message displays, click the Reply button.

3. Type your subject and your message.

4. Click the Browse button and locate and select the file on your computer.

5. Click the Open button.

   The file name displays in the Browse text box.

6. Click the Attach File button to display the Attach Files window.

   The file name and file size display below the Attach File button.

7. Click the Post button to post the message and the file attachment to your Discussion message.

   You can attach multiple documents to a single message by repeating steps 4 through 6.

MANAGING MESSAGES WebCT provides several options to assist with organizing and managing Discussion messages. These options include marking all or selected messages as read, marking selected messages as unread, and searching messages. You may search messages by a full name or user name of the message writer, thread subject, unique message number, date that the message was sent, or the content of the message. The Compiling and Downloading feature allows you to select Discussions messages, compile them into one file, and download the file.

Marking All Messages as Read

1. Click the topic in the Discussions Topics table that contains the messages that you want to mark as Read.

2. When the Discussion Messages window displays (Figure 19 on page 16), select the messages you want to mark as read.

   By default, only unread messages are listed. Click All Messages to view all messages.

3. Click the Mark all as read button.

Marking Selected Messages as Read

1. Click the topic in the Discussions Topics table that contains the messages you want to mark as read.

2. When the Discussion Messages: Main window displays, select the messages that you want to mark (Figure 19).

   By default, only unread messages are listed. Click All Messages to view all messages.

3. Click the check box to the left of the message(s) that you want to mark as read.

4. Click the Apply to selected message(s) below box arrow and select Mark as read in the list.

5. Click the Go button.

Marking Selected Messages as Unread

1. Click the topic in the Discussions Topics table that contains the messages you want to mark as unread.

2. When the Discussion Messages: Main window displays, select the messages that you want to mark (Figure 19).

   By default, only unread messages are listed. Click All Messages to view all messages.

3. Click the check box to the left of the message(s) that you want to mark as unread.

4. Click the Apply to selected message(s) below box arrow and select Mark as unread.

5. Click the Go button.

Searching Messages

1. Click the topic in the Discussions Topics table that contains the messages you want to search. If necessary, click the All link if you are not sure which topic contains the message you want to search.

2. Click Search to display the Search Topics window (Figure 25).

3. To select the search parameters, click the Topic box arrow and click the topic to search in the list. Click the Show box arrow and click All or Unread. Click the Filter box arrow and click the filter type in the list.

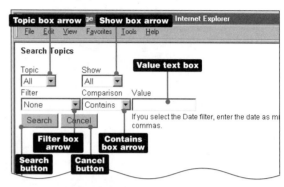

FIGURE 25 Search Topics Window

The filter types available in the Filter list are None – no filter; Name – full name of the message writer; User ID – user name of the message writer; Subject – the thread subject; Message No – the unique message number associated with each message; Date – the date that the message was sent; Message – any of the words in the text of the mail message.

4. Click the Comparison box arrow and click the desired comparison measure in the list.

The Comparison list indicates how the information that is entered in the Value text box will be compared with the filter. The Comparison measures are Contains – retrieves messages that match any part of the text or numbers entered in the Value text box; Equals – retrieves messages that match exactly the text or numbers entered in the Value text box; Before – used in combination with the Date or Number filter, retrieves all messages before the date or number entered in the Value text box. Used in combination with a filter (Name, Subject, Message), retrieves all messages containing letters that occur alphabetically before the word entered in the Value text box; After – used in combination with the Date or Number filter, retrieves all messages after the date or number entered in the Value text box. Used in combination with a filter (Name, Subject, Message), retrieves all messages containing letters that occur alphabetically after the word entered in the Value text box; Starts with – used in combination with a filter (Name, Subject, Message) retrieves messages with words that begin with the letter entered in the Value text box; Ends with – used in combination with a filter (Name, Subject, Message) retrieves words that end with the letter entered in the Value text box.

5. Type the words or numbers to be searched in the Value text box.

If you have selected the Date filter, type the date in the format dd,mm,yyyy. Include the commas.

6. Click the Search button, and then close the Search Topics window to return to the Discussion Messages window.

The Discussions Messages window displays a listing of all messages that satisfy your search requirements. After searching your messages, you may compile and download them.

Compiling and Downloading Discussion Messages

1. Click the topic in the Discussions Topics folders table that contains the messages you want to compile and download.

2. When the Discussion Messages: Main window displays, select the message(s) to download (Figure 19 on page 16). Click the All Messages link to choose from all the messages. Click the Show Unread link to choose from all the unread messages.

3. Select the order in which the messages will be presented. Click the Unthreaded link for chronological order. Click the Threaded link for threaded order.

4. Click the Apply to selected message(s) below box arrow and click Compile in the list.

5. Click the messages to be compiled in the list of messages. Click the Select all button to select all messages. Click the check box to the left of the sender's name to select individual messages.

6. Click the Go button to display the compiled messages.

7. Click the Download button to display the File Download dialog box.

8. Click Save this file to disk, and then click the OK button.

9. Select the location on your computer in which to save the file and click the Save button.

10. Click the Close button when the download is complete.

Chat

Chat is real-time communications among you, your instructor, and classmates. WebCT includes six chat rooms. Four are general-purpose rooms, one room is exclusively for use with your particular course, and one is a general chat room that allows communication among students in any course on the WebCT server. A conversation requires a minimum of two people in the same chat room.

Your browser must be JavaScript enabled to participate in and use Chat. Refer to page 3 for Browser Settings.

Accessing a Chat Room

1. Click the Communication Tools icon on the Homepage to display the Communication Tools organizer page.

2. Click the Chat icon to access the Chat rooms.

   The Chat window displays as shown in Figure 26.

3. Click a Room button to enter a room.

   The Chat applet starts and the Conversation Text Box displays (Figure 27 on the next page).

4. Click in the message text box, type your message, and press the Enter key.

   All messages and replies display in the Conversation Text Box as shown in Figure 27. The room occupants frame to the right displays the names of those who currently are in the room.

5. Click Entry Chime to be notified when someone new enters the room.

6. Click the Quit button to quit and close the window.

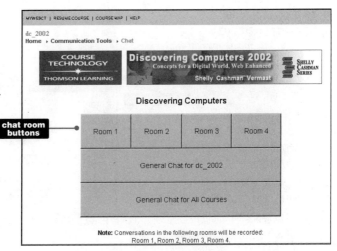

FIGURE 26 Chat Rooms

Whiteboard

The **Whiteboard** allows a group of course participants to share dynamically a graphical interface similar to a paint program. You can draw lines, create filled and unfilled objects, and modify and move objects. You also can add text and copy and paste graphics. This tool is useful for discussions where diagrams are needed.

Accessing the Whiteboard

1. Click the Communication Tools icon on the Homepage to display the Communication Tools organizer page.

2. Click the Whiteboard icon to display the Whiteboard window.

Your browser must be JavaScript enabled to participate in and use the Whiteboard. Refer to page 3 for Browser Settings.

3. Click the Start Whiteboard button.

The Whiteboard starts and the Whiteboard window displays (Figure 28). The window is divided into four sections: The icon panel on the left side, containing all the Whiteboard tools; the drawing area in the middle; the Current Users and Information boxes on the right side of the window; and cursor coordinates, line thickness and font type choosers, image selector, and foreground/background color chooser at the bottom of the window.

4. Point to any of the tools on the icon panel to display a description of the tool in the Information box.

The tool in row 1, column 1 on the icon panel clears the drawing area. The top four rows contain seven different drawing tools: text, freehand line, straight line, empty oval, filled oval, empty rectangle, and filled rectangle. Modification tools are located in the bottom four rows and include unfill, fill, reshape, modify, move, delete, and paste.

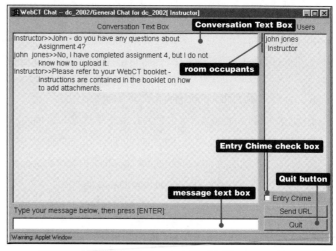

FIGURE 27 Chat Window with Messages and Replies

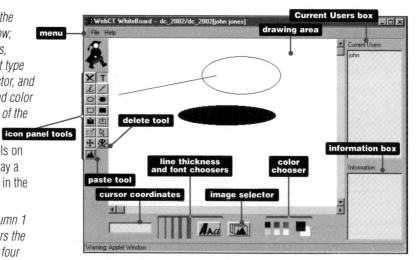

FIGURE 28 Whiteboard Window

5. Click one of the drawing tools and draw a shape on the Whiteboard.

   When you release the mouse button, your drawing displays on all participants' Whiteboards.

6. Click the delete tool, located on the seventh row of the icon panel, to delete a selected object.

7. Click the paste tool on the last row of the icon panel to paste an image.

8. Click the File menu to Load, Save, or Refresh the drawing area.

9. Click the Help menu and then click Help Contents for a comprehensive Help file.

10. Click the File menu and then click Close to close the Whiteboard.

STUDENT TOOLS

WebCT provides a variety of student tools you can use to help manage your course materials. These tools include Assignments, Calendar, Content Compiler, Grades, My Progress, Search, Glossary, Student Presentations, and Student Homepage.

Accessing Student Tools

1. Click Student Tools on the Homepage.

   The Student Tools organizer window displays (Figure 29). Your course may not contain all of these tools.

Assignments

Assignments allows your instructor to post a list of assignments for your course. Once the assignment is submitted, your instructor assigns a grade to your completed work. The grade is posted to the gradesheet automatically. To submit more than one file for a specific assignment, you must repeat this submit assignment process.

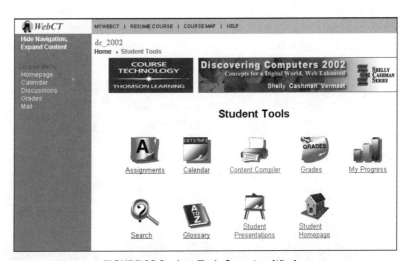

FIGURE 29 Student Tools Organizer Window

Submitting Assignments

1. To upload completed assignments, click the Assignments icon.

   The Assignments window displays (Figure 30).

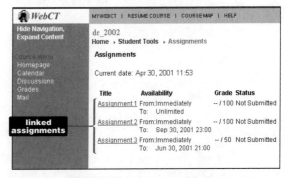

FIGURE 30 Assignments Window

2. Click the linked name of the assignment you want to submit.

   The Assignment window displays instructions and information (Figure 31).

3. Click the Student files button.

   The Student Files for Assignment window displays (Figure 32). In this window, you begin the upload process for your assignment(s).

4. Click the Upload button.

   The Upload File for Assignment window displays. In this window, you continue with the upload Student Files for Assignment process.

5. To locate the file, click the Browse button to open your computer's choose file dialog box.

6. Locate and click a file to select it.

   The Upload File for Assignment window redisplays with the name of the file in the Filename text box (Figure 33).

7. Click the Upload button to upload the file.

   The Student Files for Assignment window redisplays with the uploaded file name displaying in the Student files table (Figure 34).

8. Click the Return to Assignment link to redisplay the Assignment window (Figure 31).

9. To submit the assignment, click the Submit assignment button.

   The Submit Assignment window displays. If your instructor has enabled WebCT's e-mail notification feature, you can receive e-mail notification outside of WebCT that your assignment was submitted successfully. Type your personal e-mail address in the text box. If your instructor has not enabled the e-mail notification feature, this text box will not display.

10. Click the Submit assignment button. Then click the OK button when the confirmation dialog box asks you to confirm the procedure.

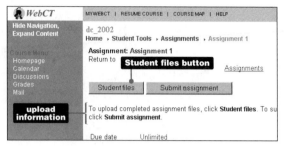

FIGURE 31 Assignment Window

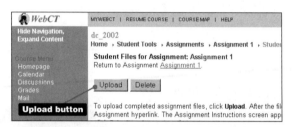

FIGURE 32 Student Files for Assignment Window

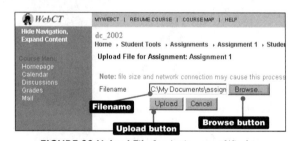

FIGURE 33 Upload File for Assignment Window

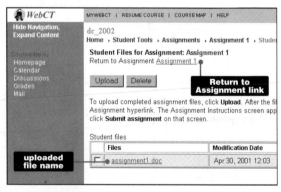

FIGURE 34 Student Files - File Uploaded Window

The assignment is submitted and the Assignments window redisplays, with the Status changed from Not Submitted (Figure 30 on page 23) to Not Graded. When the assignment is graded, the Status changes to Graded, and your grade displays in the Grade column. Click the Graded link to view your instructor's comments about your work.

FILE NAMES AND EXTENSIONS WebCT will not recognize file names with spaces, or characters that are not numbers or letters. Add a file extension that corresponds to the software you used. For example, if you completed your assignment in Word, add .doc to the file name if the software program does not add it automatically.
The file name cannot contain any of the following characters:

- spaces, tabs, line feeds, carriage returns
- : ~ [ ] ! @ # $ % ^ & * ( ) + ` } } | \ < > , ? / ; ' "

Calendar

You and your instructor can use the **Calendar** like a daily planner. Your instructor may post due dates for assignments, presentations, quizzes, and other scheduled events. A list of newly added events displays each time you access the Calendar. You can use the Calendar for your private entries as well, visible only to you, and you can download and compile a list of calendar events.

Accessing and Using the Calendar

1. Click the Student Tools icon on the Homepage to display the Student Tools organizer page (Figure 29 on page 23).

   Some Course Technology Web courses also may have the Calendar icon on the Navigation Bar.

2. Click the Calendar icon.

   The Calendar displays as shown in Figure 35.

3. Click the month box arrow and then click the month to edit in the list.

4. Click the linked number that corresponds to the day of the month to which you want to add or edit an entry.

   The Calendar window displays the day of the linked number you clicked on the Calendar (Figure 36).

5. Click the Add entry button.

   The Add a Calendar Entry window displays (Figure 37 on the next page).

6. Fill in all required text boxes and other optional boxes as needed.

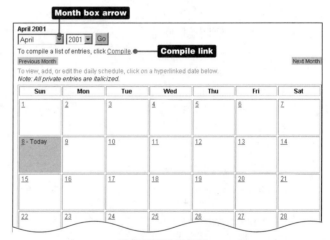

FIGURE 35 Calendar

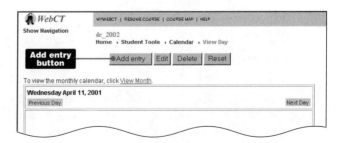

FIGURE 36 Calendar View Day Window

7. If necessary, click the Access level private button.

   The default for students is private. Making public entries requires that your instructor change the default.

8. Click the Add button to enter the information into your calendar.

9. Click the Add entry button to add another entry and select a different date.

10. When you complete your entries, click the Calendar link to return to your Calendar and view your entries.

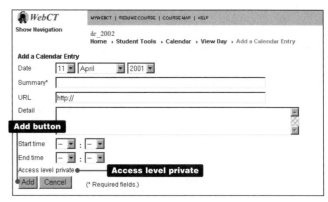

FIGURE 37 Add A Calendar Entry Window

Compiling a List of Calendar Events

1. Click the Compile link (Figure 35 on the previous page).

   The Compile Calendar Entries window displays (Figure 38). Use this feature to assemble a list of public events for a specified time period.

2. Click the appropriate box arrows to select From and To dates.

3. If you are looking for special events, use the Filter feature.

4. Click the Display button to view your compiled list.

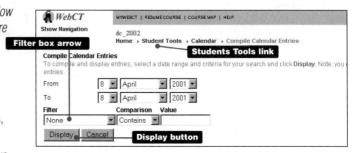

FIGURE 38 Compile Calendar Entries Window

5. Click File on the menu bar and then click Save As. Click the Save button to save the file on your computer.

6. Click the Student Tools link to return to the Student Tools organizer page.

Content Compiler

The **Content Compiler** allows you to create a custom collection of course notes from the topics in a Content module. You can print the pages, view them online, or save them as a file.

Compiling a Set of Pages

1. Click the Student Tools icon on the Homepage to display the Student Tools organizer page (Figure 29 on page 23).

2. Click the Content Compiler icon.

   The Content Compiler window displays (Figure 39). This window consists of a list of all content modules contained within the course.

3. Click the option button to the left of the section of the content module you want to compile.

4. Click the Compile button to display your selection in the Content Compiler window (Figure 40).

5. Click the check box to the left of the page(s) you want to compile.

   Clicking the Mark All button selects all pages at one time.

6. Click the Compile button.

7. View your pages online, print your pages, or use the File Save option in your browser to save the compiled pages.

   Information on printing is provided on page 32.

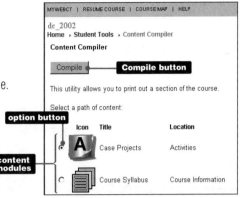

FIGURE 39 Content Compiler Window
Displaying List of All Content Modules

Grades

Grades allow you to view your own grades. Some examples of grades you might see are test or quiz results, an instructor-entered grade, an assignment grade, or a calculated grade.

Accessing and Viewing Grades

1. Click the Student Tools icon on the Homepage to display the Student Tools organizer page (Figure 29 on page 23).

2. Click the Grades icon to view your grades.

   A spreadsheet-type window containing your grades displays. If the number of columns is greater than what displays in one window, use the horizontal scroll bar to view the other columns.

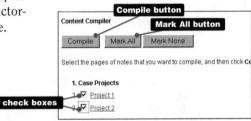

FIGURE 40 Content Compiler Window
with List of Selected Content Modules

3. When you are finished viewing your grades, click the Student Tools button to return to the Student Tools organizer page.

My Progress

My Progress allows you to see a list of the pages you have visited. Listed also is total number of pages visited, your last login, and the last page visited. Your instructor has access to this information.

Accessing and Viewing My Progress

1. Click the Student Tools icon on the Homepage to display the Student Tools organizer page (Figure 29).

2. Click the My Progress icon to display the Student Profile page and Distribution of Visits.

3. Click Show History of the Content Pages Visited to display history.

4. Click the Student Tools button to return to the Student Tools organizer page or the Home button to return to the Homepage.

Search

You can use **Search** to locate specific text within a course. This text may be from content modules within a path, an index, or Discussions postings. Only the tools within your course will be available as an option.

Using the Search Tool

1. Click the Student Tools icon on the Homepage to display the Student Tools organizer page.

   The Search tool also may be available on the Content module ACTION MENU or on other organizer pages of your Course Technology WebCT course.

2. Click the Search icon.

   The Search the Course window displays.

3. Click the Search box arrow and then click the type of content you want to search.

4. Click the Contains text box and type the word or phrase to search.

5. Click the Search button to display your search results.

   The search results display as shown in Figure 41. You can access any of the linked items quickly by clicking the linked title names.

6. Click the Student Tools link to return to the Student Tools organizer page or click the Home link to return to the Homepage.

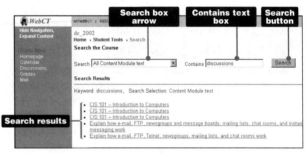

FIGURE 41 Search Results Window

Glossary

The **Glossary** allows you to search glossary entries. Your instructor may have designed your course so you can access the glossary by clicking the Glossary icon or by clicking a highlighted word in a content page. The Glossary also may be available on the Content Page ACTION MENU. When using the Glossary, you have the option to list the entire glossary, list glossary entries by the first letter, or search the glossary for a particular keyword.

Using the Glossary

1. Click the Student Tools icon on the Homepage to display the Student Tools organizer page (see Figure 29 on page 23).

2. Click the Glossary icon.

   The Glossary window displays (Figure 42).

3. Click one of the letters of the alphabet to view glossary entries by the starting letter.

4. Click the View All link to view the entire glossary, starting with the letter A.

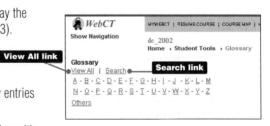

FIGURE 42 Glossary Window

5. Click the Search link to display the Search text box and to search for a keyword. Type `computer` in the Enter a search term text box.

6. Click the Search button to search for the term, computer.

   The Glossary returns every keyword in which the definition contains the word, computer.

7. Click the Student Tools link to return to the Student Tools organizer page or click the Home link to return to the Homepage.

Student Presentations

Student Presentations allows you to upload files to your WebCT course. Generally, the instructor designates this tool for group projects. You can view other student group presentations as well as your own. Your instructor must create the groups before you can use this tool. Groups can consist of one or more students.

Your instructor will provide information on how to use your software to create your presentation. Keep in mind the name of your file must be index.html. Your instructor also may suggest that you **compress**, or **zip**, your presentation for easy upload and will provide information on how to create a zipped file.

A presentation is published in two steps: first, you use your computer and create the presentation as a set of linked HTML pages, then you upload it to WebCT. Your instructor will provide information on how to create your presentation.

Using Student Presentations

1. Click the Student Tools icon on the Homepage to display the Student Tools organizer page.

2. Click the Student Presentations icon.

   The Student Presentations window (Figure 43). The Student Presentations window lists all the groups in the class. An Edit Files link displays to the right of the name of your group(s).

3. Click the Edit Files link to display the Manage Files window (Figure 44).

4. Click the Upload file option button, and then click the Go button located beneath File Options.

   The Upload File window displays.

5. Click the Browse button, locate and select the file on your computer, and then click the Open button. You will have to upload your presentation one file at a time.

   Note: If you want to upload multiple files at once, zip them first using WinZip (PC), ZipIt (Mac), or another file compression application and then upload the .zip files.

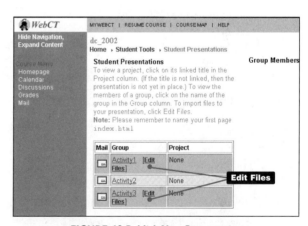

FIGURE 43 Publish Your Presentation

FIGURE 44 Manage Files Window

6. When the Upload File window displays with the name of your file in the Filename text box, click the Upload button.

   The Manage File window displays, and the uploaded file shows as a link below your presentation group folder (Figure 45). If your files are zipped, click the option button to the left of the zipped file; click the Edit box arrow and select Unzip. Click the Go button to unzip your file.

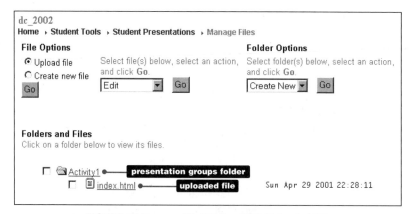

FIGURE 45 Manage File Window With Uploaded File

7. Click the file link to view the file.

8. Click Home to return to the Homepage.

Student Homepage

If your instructor provides the **Student Homepage**, you can create your own personalized Web page within your WebCT course. You can add text, graphics, and pictures, and even link to other Web sites. You can view your Homepage and the Homepage of others in your class.

Creating Your Homepage

1. Click the Student Tools icon on the Homepage to display the Student Tools organizer page.

2. Click the Student Homepages icon.

   The Student Homepage window displays. The left frame contains your linked name, and the right frame is empty.

3. Click your name to display the Student Homepage window.

4. Click the Help button to display a WebCT Help page with step-by-step instructions on how to create your Homepage.

5. Print this page and use it as a guide to create your page.

6. When you have finished your Web page, click the Student Tools link to return to the Student Tools organizer page or click the Home link to return to the Homepage.

ASSESSMENT

Assessment consisting of online testing and instant feedback for multiple choice and true/false questions are WebCT's main features. Short answer and fill-in-the-blank questions also are available. These types of questions generally require an instructor response before the grade is submitted.

Full and Single Quiz Lists

You can access a full quiz list or a single quiz list. Your instructor determines the type of access. A **full quiz list** displays every quiz in your WebCT course. Each quiz will have a title, date of availability, duration or time limit, grade, an indication if the quiz has been completed, and the number of attempts. A **single quiz list** shows only the quiz to be taken.

Your instructor determines the date and time of availability, the number of attempts, and the time limit. The quiz title will not link if it is not available or the number of previous attempts is greater than that specified by the instructor. In addition to your regular quizzes, you may have practice quizzes or self-tests.

Using the Full Quiz List

1. Click the Assessment Tools icon on the Homepage.

2. When the Quiz window displays, click the linked quiz name.

The Quiz Introduction window displays. This window contains detailed instructions on how to take the test. Read these instructions carefully. Time begins to accrue the moment you click the Begin quiz button. If your quiz is timed, make sure you are ready.

3. Click the Begin quiz button.

The quiz starts in the Quiz window shown in Figure 46.

The left frame contains the test questions and a Save answer button following each question. The right frame contains a table with

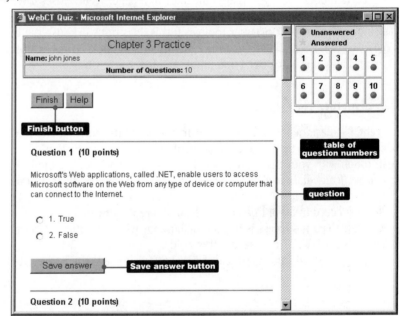

FIGURE 46 Quiz Window

the question numbers. Directly below each question number is a red circle. When you answer a question and click the Save answer button, the red circle changes to a green star. Your instructor may decide to present one question at a time instead of the entire test.

4. Read the question, click your answer, and then click the Save Answer button. Review your answers if time permits. You can change any answer, but make certain to click the Save answer button again if you change the answer.

5. When you complete the quiz, click the Finish button to display the Submit Quiz for Grading dialog box.

6. Click the OK button to display the View Results window to review your score and answers.

   Your instructor must make this option available.

7. When you finish reviewing your test, click Home to return to the Homepage.

Using the Single Quiz List

1. Click the Assessment Tools icon on the Homepage to display the Assessment Tools organizer page.

2. Click the appropriate quiz number to link to the quiz.

3. Complete Steps 2 through 7 of Using the Full Quiz List.

PRINTING

On certain occasions, you may want to print a page. WebCT uses a Web page structure called **frames**. To print a frame, make sure to click inside the frame you want to print and then click the Print button on your browser toolbar. If this does not work, use the mouse to select the information you want to print. Click File on the menu bar and click Print to display the Print dialog box. In the Print dialog box, click Selection and then click the OK button.

SUMMARY

WebCT is designed with a set of features to facilitate learning and navigation. Special tools include communication, testing and assessment, and student tools. Using the Communication tools to keep in touch with your instructor and classmates are some of the more important elements of an online course. Immediate feedback on your practice quizzes and tests is another motivational feature. Student tools help you organize your course.

To succeed in an online course is no different from succeeding in a traditional course. An important key to your success is to become familiar with the different components and features contained within your WebCT course and this guide.

For additional information about WebCT, visit the WebCT Web site at webct.com.